our cancers

A CHRONICLE
IN POEMS

Dan O'Brien

cancers

ACRE
CINCINNATI 2021

Acre Books is made possible by the support of the Robert and Adele Schiff Foundation and the Department of English at the University of Cincinnati.

ISBN-13 (pbk) 978-1-946724-42-7
ISBN-13 (ebook) 978-1-946724-43-4

Designed by Barbara Neely Bourgoyne
Cover art: Charles Emery Ross, *Moon over Magenta*, 2007, acrylic on canvas, 30 in. x 30 in.

The press is based at the University of Cincinnati, Department of English and Comparative Literature, McMicken Hall, Room 248, PO Box 210069, Cincinnati, OH, 45221–0069.

Acre Books books may be purchased at a discount for educational use. For information please email business@acre-books.com.

For Bebe,
our reason for being

On the fourteenth anniversary of 9/11—a catastrophe we witnessed firsthand, our apartment on Water Street suffused with the World Trade Center's carcinogenic dust—my wife discovered a lump in her breast. Six months after her double mastectomy, on the day of her final infusion of chemotherapy, I awoke from my colonoscopy procedure to some bad news of my own. My treatment would consist of intensive chemotherapy and two major surgeries over the next nine months.

The consecutiveness of our personal disasters, with a daughter not yet two years old at the start of it, was shattering and nearly silencing. At hospital bedsides, in hospital beds myself, and at home through the cyclical assaults of our therapies, these poems came to me in fragments, as if my unconscious were attempting to reassemble our lives, our identities and memories—of childhood, of courtship and marriage, of loved ones lost to cancer and those who had survived; as if I were in some sense learning how to speak again.

These poems have been revised in the years since, and reordered here and there, but it's my hope that the present collection conveys the trajectory of trauma, while celebrating the will of sufferers and caregivers to remain and to renew.

Dan O'Brien
December 2020
Los Angeles

I

Waking up
middle-aged
descending

to a kitchen
like the inside
of a lantern

with the babe
a flickering
babble when

you pause
at the running
faucet to ask Love

can you feel
my breast O
no O no

is all
I can say
collapsing

finally
the spark
catching

2

Another morning
sirens roused us
to the specter

of a businessman
static with ash
He was confused

where he was
On Water Street
we craned our necks

receipts cascading
the exponential rose
blooming through

the second tower
An old woman fell
to her knees O

no O no How
your tears then
scattered the road

out of the blast
breathing our choking
malediction lost

in the crush of
the multitudes
reborn from dust

Thank you
for crying
for us

3

We drove into
the deepening
blizzard

to the bar
of an inn where
I confessed

you confessed
tabletop votives
around us like prayer

then took you home
and could have
let you go

into black trees
blue snow pale moon
but followed

and turned you
around with
my voice Then

kissing in the brisk
capsule of the car
idling beside

loose farmyard walls
snowflakes occluding
breath-blearing glass

Then serpentine
the mountainside
slicing swish around

harrowing switchbacks
along a river
unfrozen within

Then climbing
indiscreet stairs
to the tall arc

of your spine
in the old bed
in the old house

as the cinders
nestled in the
cast-iron stove

wind gasping
in the rafters
In the morning

you opened
your eyes to the
bright cold room

with your wild
wide smile that asks
What's next This

early morning
eyes closing
you're whirled

away from me
into another
bright cold room where

they will excise
the ember of
your disease

You are going
where I fear I
cannot follow

4

In the dream
you haven't shared
your number

Or you have
and I must
have forgotten

where you are
So trying
every door

I surprise
couples caught
in flagrante while

others remain
adamantly
secured

The eternal
hotel requires
masks on men

ostrich feather
bandages whalebone
splints for women

I overhear
you have retired
with friends

to a corner
feathered ferns
sipping tea

When I wake
I worry you won't
recognize me

5

In the dream
we discover
our home

is much larger
than ever
we had known

I call out
This wall is
tunneling I cry

These walls are
a curtain
uncoupling to reveal

a theater
of our peers
watching us

without laughter
or tears they hold
their breath

6

Missouri
is a state
of not knowing

Why
my psychic asks
am I hearing

Missouri Missouri
Maybe I offer
my mother

because she was
almost raped
in Missouri

long ago she
once informed me
before escaping

through the trees
though she lied
desperately During

your surgery
in the packed lot
a woman

bald
beneath her
Missouri ballcap

has to be
a portent of
something surely

That night I dream
of Father in bed with
Mother who draws

a bead on me
as I flap
like a bat

in the trees
in Missouri
maybe

7

The holiday
of catastrophe
with friends

from crestfallen
adulthoods re-
convening

to say love
you maybe for
the first or

last time with
such bounded cheer
Their bouquets

accumulate
already sweetly
decaying She sobs

into the pulse
in my neck when
they are gone The young

invite our envy
as the old
deserve it like

her mother resting
in our vacant
marriage bed and

her father hiding
behind veils
of cigar smoke while

the babe leaps
barefoot stone
to stone

8

Still young
sprung
from school

spiriting up
historical steps
into the blaze

of Andalucía
you found me
waiting for your

hand in mine spiraling
into the dazzle of
the drawn room

to display
our porcelain
undress

You questioned
These breasts
big enough

for you my love
O my love
laughter

careening
into the cama
matrimonial the

only word
on my tongue was
Girl

9

The girl who snagged
the handsomer twin
you once favored

they are living
now in Paris where
she undergoes

a treatment
nearly identical
to your own

Do you recall
that evening when
after dinner

she flashed
her frying pan
advising

we request
its lustrous twin
for our wedding

I marveled at
the steel already
turning black

10

The eve
of our wedding
you stepped into

your parents' house
your family our friends
at their revels

and raised
your arms in
harmony when

the ties round your
slender neck
unraveled and

your blouse
flitted open
revealing

never
a less fitting
farewell

11

Noontime
no warning
night falls

who knows
the cause
the crime

12

Did my mother
hex our door
lamenting

the loss of that
which she had never
possessed

How long
have I expected
this gift

13

I beg you
not to mention
what is happening

over the head
of the babe
so we squabble

like parents
familiar and
alarming

at this late stage
to regress to
what maimed us

from the start
Your strength threads
the eye of

the fury
that sews sharp
seams in the

agony
that cloaks you
At dawn

a shard
of last night
bites my heel

My limp stamps
our floor like
sealing wax

14

Mother
O Mother
Mother I

call to
and from
nowhere

15

Every time
I find myself
alone

in a strange city
I imagine this
is my new home

I must find
my way
to live here

16

Will I be
the man I saw
tending the fire

in the hostel
by the bridge
by the sea

where waves
doused candles
in the gale

in the travails
of my traveling
disorder

He piled
a tin scuttle
with turf

Like me
he was doomed
to wander

though his orbit
I knew then
could not end

He murmured
with a woman wan
by the hearth

before kneeling
to feed the
licking grate

and a shriek
blew soot into
our lungs

17

The flies
hatched in
the walls

while you slept
in the night
beside me

while the snow
filled fields
with peace

while a moose
filled winter
with his breath

while mice
filled our pockets
with seeds

the flies
multiplied snarling
on our walls

so I slaughtered
the flies
for love

18

Rising in the west
determined
to forsake

the cathedral for
the chalice of
the sea

through sea-
confounding clouds
boots slopping through

flop-strewn heath
and heather bereft
of cows crows

conspiring in the
iron yews clasping
stiles and tines

for me to clamber
over hounding
always the silver-

tinting mist from
mud to breath to find
these cliffs

for the sake of
my distant love
who cannot stand

her remedy like
the stones below
punished clean

19

My life shrinks
I will share
all with you

20

Near the end
she reserved
her words

of fury for those
men whose dogs
barked her down

off her path
into spattering
fetidness they

closed in on
her frail form
fangs gnashing

She berated
those who turned
called her crazy

not the dogs
who were obeying
only nature

In the end
she prepared
her poems

of her end
walking along with
a heavy stick

21

I worked for her
the summer before
the exodus

She was soft-
spoken small children
a husband

She was pretty
though her skin
had sallowed

Had she already
received the
poison

when she gave me
a silver frog in
a black velvet pouch

an amulet
she said for the pit
of my pack When

I returned I learned
she'd passed on
her husband

small children
stunned moving
elsewhere

22

She was
the mother
I preferred

I presumed
when he cried
for his wife

as she lay dying
in their parlor
he was crying

for himself
his beloved
his children and not

the child I was
bending to whisper
goodbye

23

The babe
is playing
her body like

a drum
the bathing
babe clapping

ribcage
vulva like
a fever

wordlessly
declaiming
craving

her mother
who has taken
to bed again

The babe strokes
her father's hand as
she suckles the bottle

and her father sings
the only lullaby
he's ever known

24

In the dream
he pronounces
he is pleased

that you suffer
I suffer even
our daughter

So I shatter
the mirror and slash
poor dad in half

25

The frogs were
orgiastic in the
moon-wet woods

near the end
of our youth on
the crooked trail

We could have
parted ways as we
so often played

at severance in
the opera of
the city We grappled

instead beneath
branches in weeds
and sang

of the end
of our youth
like the frogs

26

November
somehow
believing

words can
cure this
curse but who

secreted
the cockroach
in the folds

of the babe's
white silken
bassinet who

wrapped black
round his once-
blinding body

27

The babe
cannot be
held

Her mother's
breasts throb with
their absence

True art
is nothing
but hunger

28

Another day
I choose to
carry into

another decade
purling ocean
grappling gusts

the babe squeals
delightfully
counting stairs

to her mother
who stands upon
the buzzing highway

29

On the island
sequestered
in a tempest

in a spartan
dormitory we
shoved our beds

together scrawled
crude poems in
bruising light

A poltergeist
slammed teacups
in the closet

We astonished
a naked man fresh
from the bath

perplexed ourselves
by the taupe tone
of his penis

The long-haired
lovebirds
in that furnace

of a kitchen were
finger-feeding their
puffy lips more

frozen
baby
peas

30

Another fall
I would meet you
in the street where

you could not be
as if you were
an apparition

preceding your
darling incarnation
toward me

while I kept
my bench clean
in Russell Square

bawled in a pew
beside the Third Fall
and Jesus Stripped

In the emerald booths
of Crystal Town
and Stab City

I rang and warbled
for your visit
So you come

this morning when
I see you striding
in boldest sun

when I had worried
you would sleep
forever

I do not know
if you walk to
me or from

31

The mortifying
cypresses of
Rome

lined the lanes
where vaulted
horizons encased

the ruffling
bulbs displacing
their smear of seed

mechanical bees
motoring round
ruinous hives

You led me
to the hush of
the shut door

the toy paws
skittering in
the gleam

you soothing
my injuries
with art

32

Is it under
the strata of
heredity

Or could it be
childhood's
cankered harvests

The mother
whose hairless head
I kissed in bed

The towers'
pulverized
miasma

The vermin
you dawdled
to decimate

Your ambition
my ambition
denaturing

The pleasurable
arguments dissecting
our resentments

The mother
who succumbed
the weekend we wed

This woman
that woman whose
deaths I versed

Did I lure
the torturer nearer
I am sorry more

sorry than you
can bear
to hear

33

Sunrise warmed
the convent walls
while you dozed

Provençal ale
perfumed a
bounteous pantry

the red clay roof
tiles prickling
like flirted skin while

beneath you
in the garden
I counted myself

a rich man in
a house we rented
for a time

34

Look there
is a spider
on the wall

O there
is the spider in
our hall now

This spider
will devour
our flies

so let
our spider
crawl

35

The brush
ensnares
her hair

her hair
floats in
the trash as

she tapers
back into
the gloom

36

What wakes me
is language
expiring

with you
if you do
When

I dream
of speaking
my mouth

muzzles dry
heaving an
omen

37

The cusp
of the century
we escaped

our hovel's
hissing heat
for the release

of snowing streets
where the ruby-
cheeked eyes streamed

behind smoked glass
entwining flutes
to the romance

of redemptive
aspirations
Encircling

the snowing square
we found our
footprints erased

38

Everything
given
goes

not from
dust to
dust but flesh

into flesh then
flesh failing into
dung

The bush
burns
in deed

Again
she rises
from bed

disgraced She forgets
She wavers
before us

voiceless Stay
reply love
refuse

39

Her hair
sloughs from
her scalp as

she braids
the babe's
copper curls

40

Do not
despair
remember

if her mother's
swept away
to heaven

once they danced
together naked
in a desert

shower her shadow
within her
shadow

41

When
you wake
from sleep

you wake
from death
you know

42

Your sex
blank as a
seashell

43

Why could it not stay
the May Day of
the green spires

of mountaintops
announcing horns
sounding a tabernacle

in Canaan all
unto myself
lackadaisically

balladeering with
my hand upon
the steering wheel

coasting through
crossroads beneath
celestial signs

pointing toward the
unforgivable
engagement

44

I cause
myself
to bleed

for you
instead
of you

Pity
plumes in
the bowl

45

Lonely
for women
I wrote

The phone
my dear was
too dear

Letters were
a literary
currency

of cunning
braggadocio
haggling for

your heart-
wringing folded
missives

fluttering flat
into my grief-
dotted lap

Patience
only to span
the vastness

46

In Florence
panting spent
combined

our minds were
untying not talking
Nothing happening

Everything will
we trusted
as the grandmothers

griped and punched
their rugs on their
balconies yawning

47

We abandoned
our families
absconding

to the bower
of rude buds
bobbling in

the reflecting
bay window in which   .
friends in flower

applauded us as
we kissed We bowed
embarrassed

I woke alone
in the wrong bed
in the farmhouse

guitars accompanying
the smoldering
pondside heap

Woke again
to their smashed
staggering shapes

chuckling shushing
hall to wall like
the elderly

we were already
becoming before
stumbling

hilariously
down the
unlit stairs

48

The quake
on the island
on our honeymoon

our bungalow
atop the ravine
walloping

our bodies
like effigies
of wet clay

melding fervently
to each other's
weight We are waiting

for the quake still
on the island
of our marriage

to snuff us or
to slumber
again

49

Salthill
pen down
promenading

the convoluting
strand into town
toward the nightly

pint the plot of
an epic before
wayfaring back

in spittle shame
rain-faced and anxious
I would pay

for every breath
wasted O waiting
for you

50

Spring and
the cricket
trills

inside
the house
The babe

ponders
the window's
talking pane

Your temples
regrow in
cobweb tendrils

I am aging
faster than
the seasons

The balm
of childsong
naturally

51

I
become
you

Whereas
before I was
your angel now

I fall unfurling
into the cruel
enfolding

knowledge of what
may come
Again we must

behold
the dreadful
faces of friends

appearing
deceptively
untouchably

revolving in
the well of the
whirlpool

52

The surgeon
is an amateur
composer

promising
in his windowless
examination cell

to force my flesh
into latticelike
madrigals

This surgeon
prescribes
caravaning to an

oasis
copious with
palms and ghosts

This surgeon
encourages adoring
like children again

This surgeon reads
the map of my
purgation

Let me heal you
he says See
these marks

I instruct you to
wash them all
away

53

The oncologist
lathers his hands
Nine months

he estimates until
we deliver your
death or life

54

I blurt
your name
vomiting

as they plunge
the pike into
the black

bile below In
the Dilaudid
dream I am seeing

souls slipping
down muddy banks
to the Styx

reversing scuffling
in the flux mercifully
I am transported

to a station
like Grand Central
Terminal churning

souls noticing
me noticing them
I wonder

where in the world
is everybody
going

55

Which was worse
lying in bed
afraid

I would open
my eyes to
my family

or to the
empty
room

56

Any stranger
may be
an angel

in the guise of
a nurse who
embraced me

in memory of
a daughter who is
for this reason alive

or this nurse
who hooked me
in his tattooed arm as

I swooned like
a relief
of the descent

from my gurney O
every stranger
can be

57

The split body
remembers
running

around the bay
toward twilight
whacks of sun

distracting my
radiating pangs
of lust of flight

chasing the
billowing ruffling
alcove of shade

veins reining
heart beckoning
the way until the

panoramic curve
atop the dune blue
foil of sea

beyond the dell's
tittering scrub
exhaling wind-

quivering limbs
Remember I said
running

58

Are we sentenced
or saved God
knows I moan

like the babe
I do not want
to go

59

Last night
my love
I longed

to reach across
to where
you lay

I lay
beside you
awake

in the womb
of our common
malady

I did not
for fear
you would feel

my fear
of losing
touch

60

After another
hurricane
of a lifetime

the earth was
piled tidily
beside a grave

like a trapdoor
plummeting into
forgetfulness heels

sinking in
the flooding lawn
remnant rain

blackening black
suits dresses trenches
despite our motley

umbrellas jostling
congregating so
feebly asking

can we leave how
can we with
the mother

shaking her head
at her daughter's
closed box

61

Will these words
be my voice
haunting you

62

What else
can the babe
apprehend

as she fondles
the bubo
of my port

asking When
will it heal
away

Away away
she used to sing
as I strolled her

beneath the moon
home to bath
and sleep

Shoulder of snow
ringlet wound
round my finger

I will give all
to keep her
so

63

The old poet
twisted astride
his idling tractor

The scar shone
in his neck like
a millipede

as he tossed
cords of brittle
beech down to me

rasping bitterly
about every enemy
under his sun

I have heard
he has not ceased
making music

64

Thinning
or not gaining
teachers asked me

Are you ill and
sometimes I was
remanded

to the displeasure
of my mother
because my pallor

was too much The truth
was I could not take
what she cooked

or was there
not enough to
go round

Until one evening
they surrendered
their sugar

to me paying
their son his loving
ransom

65

The old poet
told the young poet
You must live

through hell
once or twice
more

The young poet
smiled to be
polite

66

Midnight
we revisit
the abysmal

spasming fluids
the putrid clog
that gapes its

humors pouting
the slit
that spurts

The resident rips
my catheter out
like she's rooting

a rattler
from its den
apparently devoid

of any feeling
for my howling I
who have never

even broken
a bone yet
here I am

made one of them
sudden denizen
of this the

simultaneous city
where the unwell
crowd the under-

ground a chorus
of blackout drunks
blaspheming

a princess groaning
in the throes of
influenza while

a crone is
receiving her
devastation beside

a wood nymph with
an ankle snapped
bouldering

Look at them
remarks my wife
about a family with

a newborn needing
a feeding tube
They almost seem

content to fold
their blanket humming
a tune from some

fairy tale when
the mangled body
of a bewildered girl's

yanked salvaged from
the ambulance's
clanging maw

Help me
she's imploring
contorting

upon the
rotating kicking
clawing at her

healers who must
beat her and bind her
to save her

life persisting
in reality
violently

67

A dime
is on the
floor Look there

is another
in the carpet
calling to mind

when a single dime
in the pocket was
a token of

reassurance
from the departed
to the traveler so

we toe
our dime beneath
our sickbed

68

Only
a mother
can help

But what if
one's mother was
helpless

Too much time
has unspooled since
we last spoke

or looked
each other eye
to eye

The desolation
I am resisting
is reminiscent

of bedtimes
when she sang
to my sister

while I crouched
at the gate
attentive

as if one
can hold onto
a voice

69

Illness is
crying out for
Mother

who does not come
to the crib as
darkness swallows

The child
has learned
his lesson

70

Is there
no air
to breathe

The hours
rearrange
the shadows

My wife
flees from
my reek

The world
should break
but won't

71

Even then
I understood
when I cleaved

to your breast
shipwrecked I spied
the whale's eye

rolling against
its caul of
sea

72

The couple
in bed
above us

in our bed
in the streetlight
through frayed blinds

slapped and stabbed
each other with
their words

Their blame was
a suffocating
cesspool

We never heard
a shriek and thump
then silence

but we augured
that murder was
in their stars

Why couldn't they
disengage
emigrate

untraceably to
opposing
antipodes

O no ardor is
not what it was
we shuddered

in our bed
making love
in the streetlight

through frayed blinds
until a neighbor
pounded on our wall

73

Dear child
our hope is you
will not need to learn

the secret we
have had to keep
from you

our one
believing
child

74

Sundays
in Ireland
all that fall

I'd walk
because Jesus
what else

can one do
when life locks
itself into a

bird-streaked
bronze bust of
Michael Collins

hidden amid
the alien moss
the old world's

derision roaring
delicious behind
cracked shutters

The same panic
bedevils me
today as when

the wind
educated the ivy
in the quadrangle

and I lingered
another notch in
confinement

75

The old poet
told the young poet
We endeavor

to construct
a bridge back to
our sound mind

then handed me
his handsaw and
his ladder to curtail

the wayward limbs
in his idea
of Eden

76

Philoctetes
rocking to sleep
his unhealing heel

a castaway
not unlike me
in these damp sheets

Or the philosopher
outlasting the
displacement of

the Depression
in a cabin stacked
with stolen tomes

Whom shall I become
when I am done
taking medicine

77

I heard
the voice
in my youth

in the night
while I wept
chastising

Why do you
ignore the
open doors

of life of death
they are the same
The answer

has always been
my sin
of evasion

78

No bills no
cavities to fill no
more words No more

the hair shirt of
artistry Every
sensual

escapade
I may never
encounter Literature

sends me queasy
to the screen Concealed
from my daughter

who thinks I have gone
abroad For her
I swivel agonizingly

knotting my gown
and shuffle round
wheeling my blinking

beeping luggage
of dangling regrouping
in the numbness between

thumb-pumps of
cessation visitations
from the vampire-

phlebotomists exhaling
into the plastic
pipe to levitate

the magic ball to
forestall pneumonia
The San Gabriels

shimmering
refulgent above
the smog-striped

arterial freeways
conducting the rest
to commerce

When was my first
step after When will be
my first word

79

In the OxyContin
haze I am held
captive again

in the bedroom
of my boyhood
The dead end

outside taunts with
intimations of
the oozing brook

that fed the swamp
where we children
vanished crossing

asphalt to lush
backyards sweeping
through staked patches

plucking handfuls
of berries to smudge
our grins gruesome

and gritty stooping
beneath the nodding
candied netting of

wild grapevines
tromping our sulfurous
slash through leathery

skunk cabbage with
burrs adhering to our
cuffs knees sleeves

into the dapple
of the everlasting
elsewhere where

oily rainbowed
puddles doubled
our Otherworld

With bent matches
from toilet tanks
we conjured jade

and amethyst acrid
pyres from plastic
garbage gathered

sticks sharpened with
jackknives for war
with vaporous foes

This was the age
of milk bottles
materializing in

galvanized tin
boxes on stoops
before dawn and when

mothers threw wide
screen doors to chime
the children inside

for dinner and baths
with brass handbells
tarnished green

Innumerable nights
as we grew we saw
the faceless teens

park their cars to
smoke booze screw
then drive away

the way they came
as we would follow
in time When

am I now The crows
caw and tap
along the roof

the neighbor is
gently splashing
his new car

80

In the dream
I am still
running

81

The children
who perished
that Christmas

when we were
children acting
in New England

driving down
the treacherous
throughway from learning

Why were they gone
when we returned
to rehearse

What
is left
to do

but wait
face rapt
in the black

masking eaves-
dropping on
the chattering side

quickening
to the heart-
palpitating fright

You are alive
You are alive if
unseen until

the light
invites our
performance

82

I ache
to recollect
the future

to retreat
to the Plymouth
we sailed from or

to look through
a porthole on
a Plymouth shore

O wind wing
me toward more
tomorrows

83

In the vision
our child is
a woman

gazing across
a cozy table
at me

some locale
holy to us
like Carmel

sometime sleepy
like mid-
afternoon in this

courtyard with leaves
glinting the season
shouldn't matter

but it does
matter that
I am being

looked after
with quizzical
aggravation and

affection
I am certain
I am pleased

she contains
our features
commingling

her hair like
her mother's
copper curling

like my hair
used to like
our allusive

conversation
foundering on
the mundane

Her mother
with any luck is
running late

Our daughter
wears a dress of
Marian blue

a healer
from birth
she is why

we are here
simply sharing
a meal

84

I was broke
and Milan
posed a problem

eat
or see
The Last Supper

I squandered
my last lira
on a burger

inhaled outside
the refectory
boys balletically

footballing shoeless
in the dusty piazza
dusk looming

I will come back
I told myself Wait
you'll see

85

Mending the
sickroom springs
its trap

86

This is the year
that is not
a year

The winter was
a conflation of
grievous errors

Dull spring
yielded a few
null flowers

Dry summer
on withered thighs
tottering toward the

inevitable fall
when our child leaves
for school

I pray
for time
to pass

or not
to pass
at all

87

The day before
you told me
the end

was growing
inside you
meaning

among worse things
there would be
no siblings

we stashed our
little red wagon
in the bushes and

rambled down
to the shore
with the babe and

trudging back
we found our
little red wagon

gone O well
we consoled
ourselves

hopefully
somebody homeless
took it some-

body who can
at least
use it

88

Windfall of pennies
in the pavement some
heads up and some down

Leave them for
the next one
round

89

The longest
night of the year
she summoned me

to the mountain
to confer with her
inside her gold cage

She admitted
she coveted
my ignorance

She had been
where I would be
going She thrilled me

with stories set
above the laundry
in Temple Bar

She divorced
her fatherly
professor

Her wasting
was halted by
her madness

She loved me
intrinsically she said
flattering You

are no longer
on fire You are
the flame

as I reeled
back into the
obscurity

fumbling for
my keys
in the snow

90

She waded
through riptides
of irises

three years
before her
diagnosis

She unlocked
my temporary
sanctuary

Then spotting
a copperhead
in the driveway

she scooped it
with a branch and
flung it into

the susurrating
bulrushes
inquiring

Have I shown you
the way to
the cross

91

In the cave
on the isle
of my exile

subsisting
on moths and
exudations

I have worn
a groove
in stone

hoisting
my carcass
aloft

to listen
at the hole
for the voice

raining like ash from
sky moon stars
that whispers

of birth
upon birth
O hear

O world
all that I am
hearing

92

You say
You will live
Look at me

I am through
I am turning
farther along

the wilderness
track I am lifting
the lantern

through the fog
for you to follow
This way

93

Every day
I must make
my pilgrimage

to San Vicente
in the cool of
the Canary

Island pines
Have you seen
my crabbed gait

rippling cramps
bargaining with
each wincing tread

as summer subsides
wildfires kindling
hummingbirds

hover into the
fig tree leaves I know
I can make it if

I can make it to
San Vicente and
the half mile home

94

The old poet
died today
Predictably

the world
celebrated his
notoriety while

the young poet
envied honestly
his longevity

95

The farmer
in the window
in his wheelchair

skin scored
with lesions
head hung low

face caressed by
sun-faded
lace curtains

looked down upon
the blemished
adolescents

peddling
his produce
to housewives

While his wife
cut flowers
for her heart

and his odd son
handed flowers
to the odd girls

I juggled
tomatoes
to inspire

a smile
in the face
I desired

96

The angel
turned out to be
an old woman

in an anteroom
of exhausted
patients

awaiting
the calling of
our names who

noticed me
particularly gripped
my trembling hands

I need to give
this young man
a message

Long days
she said her face
unreadable

her fingers fragile
and weaving like
a nest

You will have
long days
on this earth

Keep trusting
How many times
did she insist

before waving
through sliding
doors wishing

everybody
here a happy
holiday

97

Rescued
from war
he confesses

sometimes
he misses it
at best

he befriended
what was lurking
there inside him

He is concerned
he may unlearn
his wisdom

How dare you
even utter
those thoughts

she scolds
We detested
every breath lost

hobbling
writhing sobbing
side by side

We are blessed
to have arrived
here alive

I am ashamed
he says Of course
you are right thinking

I am aware
now that war
never ends

98

The standing
ovation
of stones

like bones on
the beach at Nice
clattering selecting

the sleekest
for my darling to
glance across

the waves and
the waves in
Aldeburgh after

a morning's venture
along the shifting
shingle sifting

the memories
of a friend and
rival expired

retracing
the source of
the Nile

Same sound
so loud
and far

99

Once I endured
a savage flu
in a foreign room

with a view of
sea-foam twitching
like a hem again

and again The flat
around me mean
with mirth

With anvil
of desk hammer
of drink

I wrote out
the pestilence
in seclusion

until the service
when you knelt
in the mote-teeming

beam glowing
with the prospect of
our revival

100

The child
is old enough
to ask

When will
the pain
be over

When will
your healing
be done

When
will you come
out to play

with me
again
I promise

my love
soon
I will

101

There is beauty
I may never
recover

nobody can
suspend
the moment

pedaling
my bicycle
in pursuit

of my wife
on hers with
our daughter as

night falls
moon rises
daughter laughs

acknowledgments

Thanks are due to the following journals and magazines for publishing many of these poems, many in earlier iterations: *Ambit, America, And Other Poems, Antioch Review, Bad Lilies, Bare Fiction, Birmingham Poetry Review, Blackbird, Cellpoems, Cyphers, The Dark Horse, The Fiddlehead, Hanging Loose, The Interpreter's House, Magma, The Moth, North American Review, Poet Lore, Poetry Ireland Review, Poetry Wales, The Rialto, Saint Ann's Review, Salamander, Smartish Pace, Smoke, Southern Review, Stand, storySouth,* and *Sugar House Review.*

I wish to thank especially Lisa Ampleman, Shara Lessley, TJ Jarrett, and Nicola Mason of Acre Books for their numerous invaluable insights and suggestions. I am grateful also to the following editors, colleagues, and friends who have encouraged me for several years now in the endeavor of this book: Jennifer Barber, Briony Bax, Jonathan Berger, Eavan Boland, Paul Bone, Beth Bosworth, Charles Boyle, Judith Burnley, Gerry Cambridge, Adam Chiles, David Collard, Josephine Corcoran, Nia Davies, Gwyn Davies-Scourfield, Sue Davies-Scourfield, Sasha Dugdale, Jessica Faust, Mary Flinn, Jennifer Goodrich, Rob Griffith, Judith Hall, Robert Harper, Robert Hershon, Joe Hoover, David Hudson, Lori Wolter Hudson, Mead Hunter, A.B. Jackson, Luke Johnson, Terry Kennedy, Charles Lauder Jr., Ian LeTourneau, Dick Lourie, BJ Love, Rob A. Mackenzie, Martin Malone, Fiona Moore, André Naffis-Sahely, Eiléan

Ní Chuilleanáin, Rebecca O'Connor, Stephen Reichert, J.D. Schraffenberger, Christopher Shannon, George Spender, A.E. Stallings, Nano Taggart, Brant Russell, Jennifer Lee Tsai, Adam Vines, James Womack, and Natalie Young.

My deepest gratitude is of course reserved for my wife, Jessica St. Clair, whose strength is my strength and whose love is my light.